Cars and Trucks

Ladybird

beep-beep car

noisy digger

red fire engine

dumper truck

flashing police car

yellow lorry

hooting taxi

ice cream van

speeding train

blue tractor

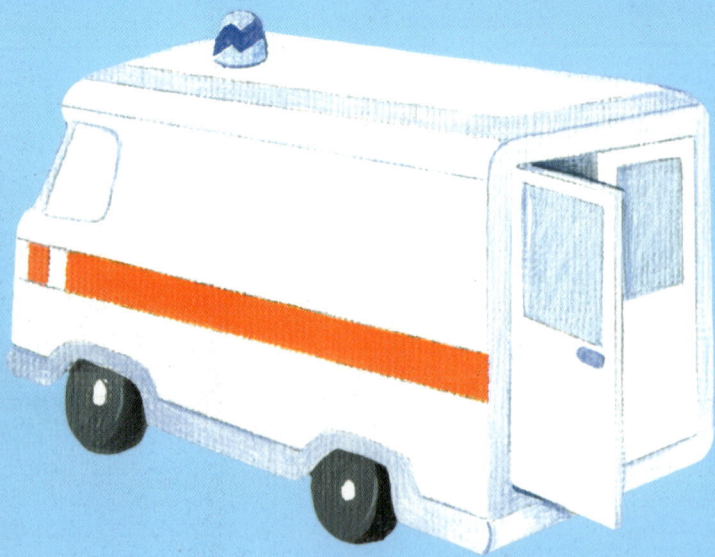

white ambulance

pickup truck

pink limousine

cement mixer

fast go-cart

huge lorry

little car

big bulldozer

rubbish truck

delivery van

long bus

green tow-truck

racing car

road sweeper

A catalogue record for this book is available from the British Library

Published by Ladybird Books Ltd
80 Strand London WC2R 0RL
A Penguin Company

2 4 6 8 10 9 7 5 3

© Ladybird Books Ltd MMV